The Open Gate

by

Clint Hancock

Copyright © 2011 Clint Hancock

All rights reserved.

ISBN-13: 978-1-105-25621-9

Thank You

I would like to thank Jessi Dawn for all she has done to complete this project. Without you this may never have gotten done. Thanks to everyone who has ever inspired me in any way. And lastly thanks to you, the reader. Without you all of this would be for not.

Drawing Pictures

I am drawing pictures
Trying to forget about yesterday
Tomorrow is just a dream
Hopefully with less screams

But the artist lives inside
With the perfect vision of the portrait
But it's never the same as he sees it

The picture is pretty and pure
Although it's never the same in the world
In the dream however it's always beautiful

Some say it's pure in London
But in reality it's blurred all over
Walk into the light for the real words are clear

Whatever

Am I alone where I stand?
They say I am loved
But when I need you, you're not there
Sometimes I wonder if you really even care

When I look at you I see a light in your eyes
But it kills me to know your flame isn't for me
Though for the sinner you call your angel
I guess I am not good for you
Is it me that you despise?

Is it my mistake, what did I do?
I try to show you love and do what's right
But I guess whatever I do is not enough for you
Are looks what makes one true to you, is it passion

Maybe I am nature's flaw
But to God I am pure and to me I am real
I don't know what makes a person real to you
But I know as jaded as things may seem I will be
fine

Great American Tragedy

I am awake when it falls
Who is the one at fault?
The victim everyone blames

It's a tragedy of death
Is it always the same?
What if the tables were turned?

Why can't we see we are killing our youth?
Violence in the home and everything we do
The world can't function without God

Then you wonder why he shoots up the school
You blame it on the music and everything you hate
Why can't you see you are at the wrong?

He is the victim here
We are the killer of all that's good
Let God return for a perfect ending

Pressure

What I need from you is understanding
But you never offered me anything besides a slap in the face

Where else could I go when I needed someone?
But you were never there for me

Tell me how I break this sickness cycled inside of me
Oh God, please help me stop the voices spinning in my head

I wish I could find a way to take back the words I said
Now I speak to you in riddles because I can't find myself

Still I pray you will return to me so I can calm myself
I am hoping for a brighter day so I can find my way back home

The search and rescue mission is not available
Now everything stops; everyone sits at home.

One Night

Give me just one night
One night for you to hate me,
Despise me, disrespect me

Let me give you a reason to overlook me
Disregard me, don't include me
If you're going to do it, you might as well have a reason

I am a real life person, believe it or not
I can break and bleed just as well as you
I could have been like you and made them feel small

But I am not like you, I choose not to be
I don't hate you, I won't hate you
I will rise above where you can't see me

I am not a rock band nor am I married to the queen
But you want to hate me and I don't know why
If you want to you can, but I will never hate you

Sweet Embrace

Every time, everyway
Every hour of everyday
I move closer to your sweet embrace

The signs of the times are evident
You can see that everyday in everyway

When I feel the ground move before me
And in my mind I see your face, I know

When the sun shines on me
My dark clouds roll away

When I can't go you gas me up
And when I'm far away, you bring me home

Remember the War

I didn't mean it
How did I hurt her?
I know how but don't see it

She pushed me too far
This time it was too much
You just can't pretend anymore

Words can cut like knives
Well I guess she didn't know when to stop
I suppose I could say the same

Now it's over, all is still
I cannot wash my hands of this act
Neither can she, nor release the blame

Forgive me for this,
I never knew the loss
Maybe next time we can make it right

Dreaming On

In the storm I wish you could see my face in the lightning
Although somehow you could tell I was here

Can you see me?
I can smell your sweet perfume, you were there

I wanted you to want me, just like I wanted you
Am I asleep again?

Dreaming on love, dreaming thoughts of you
Dreaming on wanting to be with you

Those days when nothing seems to go my way
Can you be there?

Sunshine you always seem to brighten my day
I miss you much

Here I am don't look the other way, stay awake
Why can't I stay awake?

Friend is Temporary

Don't leave me alone, because now I know
My life, my friend is temporary
I call this my home, in my room being alone

In my sorrow, and in my weakness
Now I know no one cares
It doesn't taste the same way as yesterday

You're not the same as I remember
Would you even care if I was dead?
To take these pills and lay my head

Am I forgotten by your intentions?
Stone sour and callus to the bone
I still hang by just a memory

My life long dream has been shattered
You have told me what I can't have
Friend is temporary when I need you

Why Love

Why do you let me grieve?
Why do you give me all these hardships?
I don’t understand, could this be your plan?

How is it that I have so much pain?
But you expect me to remain humble
Still I wonder do you hear my pleas.

How can I be so consumed?
Yet I am lonely and scared
Even though I try to hide the fear away

My heart cries out for mercy
When your grace and love is all I need
I still don’t understand why this curse is upon me

Why don’t I hate instead of love like I do?
The pain is nothing compared to what you went
through
I would yet do it again to be with you.

Master

An orange is to tangy
An apple is to sweet
Your love once was,
But now is soft and meek

Is this for real, or are you in it for the thrill
Can one be so sure?
Where is all the fun?

Am I a puppet on your string of life?
Can it be done?
Or is the battle yet to be won

Fate

Twisted fate
The answer lies in the young man's blood

Cream of the crop
A king he has become

In this life I have seen so many things
Many things that should not be

Corrupted is the mind,
The world is to blame
Captured is the flag

Game Over!

Unchained

In a box left unsaid
Many things inside my head

Chicken scratch in my brain
Could it be that I am insane?

Where is the pleasure of the game?
Is it real, or am I made of clay

Unchained Melody in my soul
I think I am going to lose control

Step on the brakes inside my head
Don't go away and leave me for dead

Drowning Pool

It comes after dark
Because that’s when it hurts the most

Why did you take the pill?
I don’t remember but it stings

I breathe for you
But when you turn away it kills me inside

I have been thrown down
Pushed around battered and bruised
All this talk about love brings me down

When you at look me
You see a Drowning pool
But he sees me clean

Presence

Tooth for a tooth
Eye for an eye
Take the breath from my body
My broken bones lay before thee

Choose life or death
I can't breathe this pain
As my nails lay before me
What's right from wrong?

I feel the presence,
But are you near
Maybe it's just my pride
But the anger's inside

To live another day or to love another one
The dream of playing in the sand
With the fear of standing out in the rain

Breathe the life in me
So that I can feel you close to me
Draw a picture of me
So I may stand by thee

The Real

The time has come to think
About the real
About who you are
And what you've done

Who are you?

Deep inside you know
Somewhere in the hollow of time and space
You know the enemy

You wear it well

Can love save you?
Give it a try
Let go of yourself and descend

Take the time

Free your mind and step into the light
Learn to know him and be free

Darkside of Things

Twisted up and gnarled is the hate
Like an open cut, blood escapes
The world only left to despise

Hate is brewed from the sin
Why do I take it?
Speaking the silence out loud

Slowly work my spot
Further down the spiral
Anger now the only fear

Can't breathe from under here
Screams of millions flare
Shackled and chained with fright

Can't break this pain
I don't even know why I came
To remain here in the shadow

In The Background

I am here on this earth
But you don't seem to notice
No you don't care

Your world is round
But I am square
Sure, that's just fine with me

You don't see me
But I am here
Just in the background

Do you care?
Is that what I am fighting for?
That is why I bleed

I deserve a chance
Or maybe I should stay here
Here in the Background

Only One

I feel like I am drowning
In an ocean of deceitful things
Despising everything I know
But open to suggestions

I hope someday I will find you
Maybe I already have
Your back there lurking in the shadows
Come in and change my mind

Where I can know you better
And you can see me plain
I know you're there
I feel you flowing through my veins

I guess you're the only one
You see me through the clouds
I pray you will ever see
You're the one for me

Dream

When I dream, I dream of you
Your strength and beauty get me through
But my past and what I know makes me wonder

Or is it all just a dream
I guess my mind just isn't sure
Perhaps unlike you I am a drama queen

Still you're there and I am well aware
You live in your shell and I do care
The question is where do I go from here

If peace is love and love is good
Why can't I have peace?
It's there if you're present

Still I dream of good things and you
Don't wake me up if it's all going to end
I don't want to be there if reality bends

Never say Die

To you from me
A love story would be so kind
But none seems to be in mind

Will you stay or will you go?
How am I ever supposed to know?

Can a love be so true?
Even with all the things I've done
And all the things I've seen

You seem to take me higher and lift me up above the rest
With you I am a king waiting in the wings

Like a fire fly you light up my life
Without the knowledge of what I was before
You take me as I am

This truly is a blessing
I don't know if I deserve
But I am glad I found you
And hope you stay

Search

I know nothing is as it seems
Still I call your name
It smelled kind of sweet
But still I feel the same

Honestly I don't remember what happened
But I never thought I would see your face ever
I always thought it would be easier than this
But I guess that I was wrong

And do you remember the nights we had
The memories we shared echoing inside
Sarcastic faces and beautiful places
The taste of the herbs

Change is still the culprit
It can kill us or set you free
But it leaves you wondering
Does it even matter?

High Gear

Changing the gears
Turning the heat up
It's a brand new day

Fields of green change to silver
Tomorrow is a dream

Desert eyes look my way
This rollercoaster is so tight
Holding onto nothing from yesterday

But the beat goes on
You need it so bad
The world is new

Switching into high gear
Not letting your feet touch the ground
Hold on and someday you shall fly

Wasted

What is a life if it's wasted?
What good is your youth if you killed it?

You can't live if you're dead
You can't bring back the past to change it over again

When you feel alone,
And so far from home
Know that I am here
To carry you on

When you want to get out
Escape from this world
I am your refuge
I am your shelter

When you want to die
Put your trust in me
I will save you
From an eternity of shame

The Drug

Your words are more than words
To me it's a promise
Like sweet morning dew
On flowers that you bloomed

Your holiness and majesticness
Is peace in my soul
You're my strength when I am weak
I am dead to this world

You are everything I need in life
I am addicted to your every move
And like a drug I can't get over you
I need you more and more

Like a dog to its' master
I move when you speak
Your presence is life
As you breathe into me

When I am broken
You make me clean
Take my pride away
You give me what I need

War Machine

Worn down war machine
Lay its' head to rest

Time of new dawns
As time of old fades
The fire is out,
Yet the coals are hot

Mindless actions,
Tempers flare
Is it lost?
Or is it fate

Should they burn flesh?
While the body is cold
The mind is weak
Fact or fiction

Feeling like I have no where else to go
Should I kill the soul?

High

One touch of the face
I am stunned
Taken to heaven
And back again

A look in the eye
And I am taken away
Lost in the moment
Time stands still

Beauty is thy name
What is thy will?
Patience is the key you say
Cherish the treasure

Sound of thy voice
Heavenly sounds
Angels singing perhaps
Oh the torture of it all

Lost and Found

Alas my love,
On this wiry night
We meet again,
But is it with delight?

No my love,
It's just a goodbye
To dreams
Love has died

Hearts mended
Pieces put back togather
Eye for an eye,
Does it die?

Still you are sweet
Beauty like a rose
Pure no more
Cursed be thy name

Broken, the flame has died
Still it is yet to be put out
If love lingers
Will you be there?

Shades of grey

My love for you is still unchanged
Although I wish you felt the same

I close my eyes and pray in vain
Hope to God that you will change

If this is the way it has to be
Why do I feel this pain inside of me?

As my light begins to fade
Darkness slowly invades
In my sorrow I am overtaken

As my light fades away
My last request is for the world to change
Then my light dims
Everything fades to grey

The Man of Many Faces

Tonight I looked upon the man of many faces
His eyes blood shot and skin pale as a ghost
It seems I recognize his face

He has a face of fear, it's a cold stare
Stepping without sight not knowing what tomorrow brings
Never knowing if he will rise or fall

With a new day comes the face of anticipation
Hopes for the best and tries the hardest
But in the end his dreams go up in flames and hope is in vain

At night comes the face of loneliness
He is surrounded by people but no one cares
It is dark and damp where he is

The man of many faces knows not of time
For the darkness brings out the face of it's choosing
There is no love for the man here

Radio

Why are you always the oppressor?
Trying to tie me down to things not of my concern
You try to burry me with guilt not of my own

I am no longer the student you are no longer the teacher
I won't do your job or anyone else's
I am naive no more, now the player is being played

It's your turn to die not mine
Take away your burden you've put on me
I am free of your grip now, be gone

Now you will know what its like to burn alone
Without me there to get you through
Without you there to bring me down

Victim and Crime

If I tell you a lie would it make you the better one?
To think you're a victim of your own crimes
Suffering from your own hand

The apple of your eye got stuck along the way
Now it's stuck half inside the corner of your eye
Would you like to take a bite out of your pride?
Until you're looking for a gun to hide behind

Hush. When she goes off like a rocket ship to outer space
No orbit is safe, so I will play the silent role
Because she won't stop until she's right
And it's getting so ridicules it's not worth another breath

Let her be alone in herself, because I swear she would talk to trees if it wasn't for me
Just play along and everything is better
She may not have a mind but it's not worth losing mine
If I ever had a mind at all

I am a victim of my own crimes
Am I even real or is this all in my head
Like the gun in my hand, like the skipping record in my brain
Can I even feel? Is it real?

You blamed everyone this time, but you will blame yourself in time

Realism

More than words on a script
Or a song in a tune
When you say it
It means much more to me

Ill harmonics and unspoken signals
Build the hate that I fight
The battle gets harder each day
But the One is there to pick me up

This parasite in my head
Bonded by the chains that hold me
Although the struggling grows harder each time
And the pain flows freely

Your love frees me
You're the only way to get away
Given to fly
And get a brief break from reality

Sooner or later you're going to have to face up
With you it's no problem
Without you I would be lost
You're all that really matters

Monsters

Monsters in my head
Monsters make me wish I was dead
Living inside me they burn

They tell me to kill
They tell me to steal
And give me a lack of trust

It makes me lust
It makes me cuss
Then it swells greed inside me

Monsters that are everywhere
Monsters in the air tell me lies
Saying live for me and don't ask why

God living in heaven
Ever so great and good
Glory to your name and not the monster

The Man That Sold His Soul

He gave up everything and turned away from God
For one night of sin and lustful pleasure

Imagining everything around him was not real but a game
A game of chance and he wanted to be the ace of spades

The man who sold his soul for the world died the next day
Giving up everything for which his father had paid

Now he's lost wondering why he came
To have everything, gamble and die the next day

Now the world is lost
Sitting in sin
On the tombstone it says
The world that sold its soul for sin

Cheers

Cheers to a loved one dead and gone
With hopes we will meet in the sweet beyond

Cheers to the darkness deep in my soul
With a light burning for control

Wanting to be near and praying to be close
I thank you for the life which you gave

Cheers for the love you've showed me
Humbleness of thy greeting toward thine own
brother

Cheers for a new day and the hope that it brings
And the words you say, "peace be still and obey."

Shine On

She's a twinkling star
Knows the love of the rock
Sings like a meadow lark

The greatest thing since the cliff
She smells like a fresh rose
Where the sun shines down

Wears the name
Yet speaks the language
This silent world doesn't know

Earth is a target
To miss the truth
She is sane

She is the light
That leads the path
The light to Zion

A great thing
One little star
In a world of darkness

Blue

Blue girl
I'm so blue for you
Tonight I stayed awake and cried for you

You tore my heart into
But my love will never be apart from you

I still remember the times with you
Now I am sitting at home thinking of you

You never even had the nerve to say we're through
But you never called, so I guess it's over

Now I know it must be true
My nights are lonely and my days are blue
When I am sitting and thinking of you

About the author:

Clint, twenty-nine, hails from the great state of Oklahoma, where he lives with his bird, Alexis. He has been writing for about eleven years off and on and hopes to produce more poetry books and short stories in the future.

Writing has always been a passion of his since he was younger. He has only now decided to share it in hopes that it will inspire others out there.

www.ingramcontent.com/pod-product-compliance
Ingram Content Group UK Ltd.
Pitfield, Milton Keynes, MK11 3LW, UK
UKHW041904190726
13854UKWH00003B/1088

9 781105 256219